Bygone Barrow-upon-Soar

Barry and John Wilford

To Frank and Min Wilford for taking the family from Loughborough to Barrow on 'Tommy Smacks' (Howlett's bus) during April 1945.
Adults fare 4d
Children's fare 2d

MIDLAND STATION. BARROW-ON-SOAR

View of the Midland Railway and sidings on which now stands the houses of Crossley Close. Mr John Crossley was Chief Engineer for the Railway Company when the track was widened to four lines in 1868. He lived for many years at Barrow House, which he had built but which is now demolished having stood opposite 'Jerusalem'.

© November 1981 B & J Wilford

Designed and published by
Barry and John Wilford
18 New Street
Barrow-upon-Soar
Leicestershire LE12 8PA

ISBN 0 9507860 0 4

Printed by A.B. Printers Limited, Leicester

Preface

During the past 50 years the face of Barrow-upon-Soar has changed immeasurably. With this volume of photographs and narrative we have been able to go back in time even further. We are sure it will bring back fond memories of Barrow-upon-Soar to those who remember their early life in the village and also prove of interest to the young and to newcomers to the village.

Ichthyosaurus tenuirostris
a fish-like reptile found in the limestone at Barrow-upon-Soar

Front Cover: pleisosaurus macrocephalus Owen *found in the lower lias, Barrow-upon-Soar, in 1851. This prehistoric marine reptile was common in Leicestershire 150 million years ago.*

The fossil remains are exhibited in Leicester Museum, and a replica makes a unique village sign on the traffic island, known as 'Jerusalem', at the junction of Bridge Street, High Street and South Street.

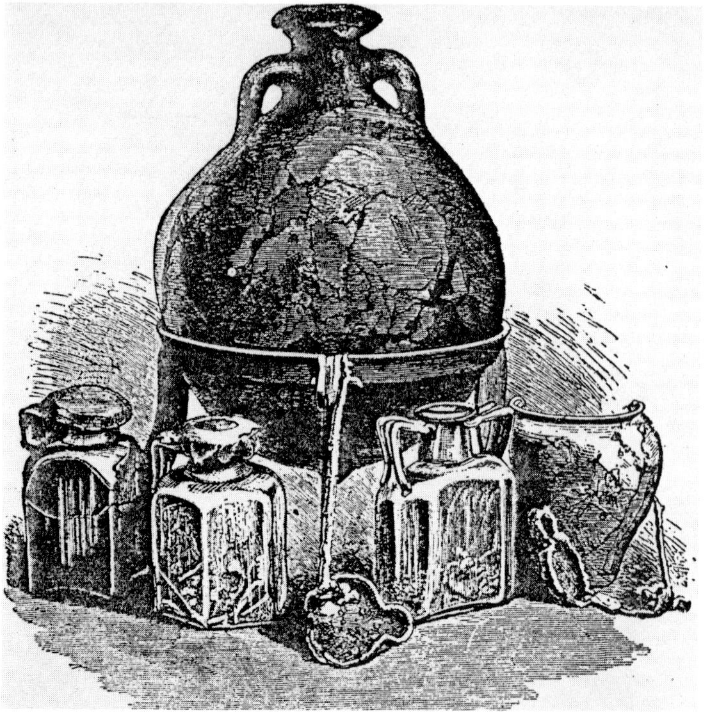

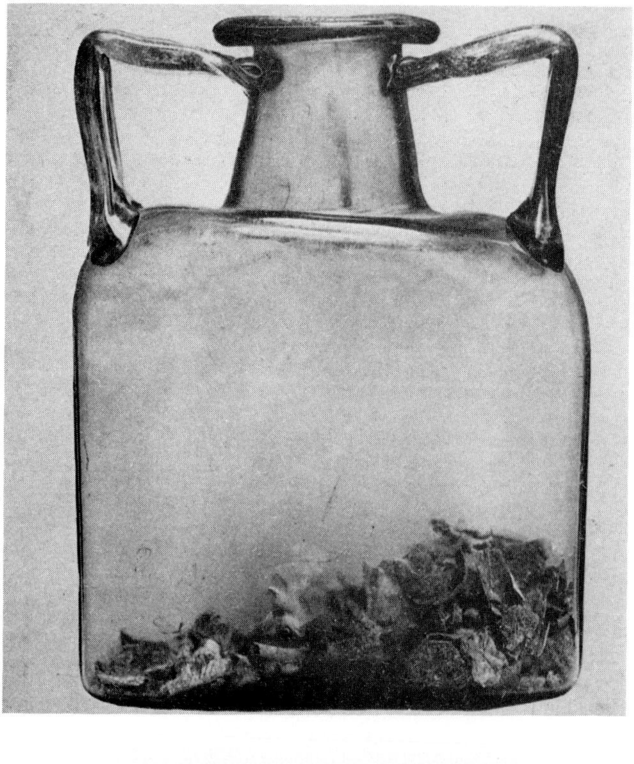

Origins

The village of Barrow-upon-Soar has had several differing names in its long past. It has been known as Barogh-on-Sore, Barow, Barewe-upon-Sore, Baro, Barrough and the entry in the *Domesday Book* is that of Barhoo, which is the derivation of the word 'Barrow' meaning a burial place.

It is virtually impossible to identify exactly who would be the first inhabitants of the village, but it could well have been the Druids who came along the Great Salt Way, which is one of the oldest roads in England, Pawdy Lane leading on to Six Hills being part of this road. The Romans most certainly came to Barrow. Whether they fortified the village is a matter for conjecture — the high ground and the river would have made it suitable for a defensive position — however the finding of Roman remains gives positive proof that some kind of settlement was erected.

In 1867 and 1874 the remains of a Roman cemetery were found adjacent to Sileby Road. The remnants contained skeletons, urns, glass vessels and other burial relics, all of these items came to light when workmen were digging for limestone in that area. The first area discovered measured ten feet by six feet and had a base made of granite rubble possibly from Mountsorrel. This is thought to have been a funeral pyre. The discovery made seven years later was oval in shape measuring 15 feet by 12 feet. Again vessels, lamps and skeletons were found, suggesting another cemetery. From these finds it could be possible that further Roman remains are still to be discovered in the vicinity. The two discoveries made in the 19th century are the most important of their kind to have been found in Leicestershire and many of the items are housed in Leicester Museum.

From 1840 to 1900 the village must have been a most exciting time for discoveries. Numerous large fossils were found when digging for limestone, not only was the famous 'Kipper' unearthed (shown on the front cover) but many others of equal merit were also found. Private collections were soon established and many items found their way to the Natural History Museum in Kensington, London, several of which are on view to the public at the time of writing.

Opposite:

Amphora, glass vessels, and Lamp, found at Barrow-upon-Soar.
Roman glass burial urn, containing human bones. Found at Barrow-upon-Soar.

John Ellis and Barrow Lime

John Ellis Esq., Chairman of the Midland Railway Co. Engraved from the original painting presented to him by a General Meeting of the Shareholders on February 18th 1858.

Lime is produced by burning chalk or limestone in a kiln. Vast quantities of limestone have been extracted from various sites in and around the village over a period of many years. It is believed that the Romans used the lime when building parts of Leicester. It was also used during Norman times and a report of the building of Kirby Muxloe Castle in 1480 refers to the use of lime from 'Barough'. By 1845 there were eleven lime delphs (open cast mines) in the parish. Indiscriminate digging took place in many parts of the village without any apparent permission being sought and no production of plans etc; this was eventually to lead to disaster over one hundred years later when the newly built Grays Court, the flats for the elderly, collapsed due to underground lime workings.

One of the major producers of lime was John Ellis who operated a driftmine near Heyhill Lane, off Sileby Road, and a large delph situated in Sileby *(pictured above)*. The burning of the lime was carried out in bottle shaped, coal burning kilns. The pungent aroma given off by these kilns could be smelt throughout the village. Many said at the time that the aromatic air in the village was the reason for people in the area being cured of consumption. Indeed at the turn of the century it was common practice for London doctors to send numbers of tuberculous patients to the village for the 'Barrow Cure'. However, the pure limestone dust at the quarry face was a killer and many of the workmen suffered from asthma and other similar bronchial complaints and only after the introduction of breathing aids were deaths avoided.

John Ellis Ltd continued to produce lime until 1925. In the meantime the company had begun to manufacture cement in the early 1900s, the lime supply for this product coming in later years from Kilby Bridge, near Wigston. The manufacture of concrete building blocks and other precast concrete goods commenced soon after, some of the first blocks to be produced were used in the building of number 231 Sileby Road, then known as 'The Firs'. Cement production ceased in about 1935 but the concrete products were still made, with the cement coming from Ketton and the aggregate by rail from the nearby Mountsorrel granite quarry.

Upon the recent acquisition of the company by Redland Ltd, the name of John Ellis has disappeared after over 100 years on the Sileby Road site.

Holy Trinity Church

The parish church is that of the Holy Trinity and there is a reference to a church on the site in the years 1135-1154 in the reign of King Stephen. The church registers, however, do not begin until 1563. A short history of the church was published in 1938 by Heywood Chiltern to celebrate the octingentenary of the church. In this booklet he describes the many and varied alterations that have taken place over the years. One major project was the rebuilding of the tower in 1868, but owing to the neglect of the builder the tower fell one week before Christmas Day of the same year, carrying with it a portion of the nave. Restoration work was started immediately and completed by 1870.

A memorial inside the church, known as the Cave Tablet, provides quizzical reading.

> 'Here in this Grave there Lyes a Cave,
> We call a Cave a Grave.
> If Cave be Grave and Grave be Cave
> Then Reader Judge I Crave
> Whether doth Cave here Lye in Grave
> Or Grave here Lye in Cave?
> If Grave in Cave here buried lye
> Then Grave where is thy Victorie?
> Goe Reader and Report here Lyes a Cave
> Who Conquers Death and Buries his own Grave.'

Holy Trinity Church, Barrow on Soar.

Theophilus Cave was an ardent churchman and his nephew Humphrey Babington (founder of the Old Men's Hospital) remembered all his life his uncle's deep devotion to the church, and in his will he provided for the supply of bibles to the poor children who could read; the words 'The Gift of Theophilus Cave Esq.' to be impressed in gold letters on the covers.

FARM BARROW

Rectory Farm (top left) once stood on the Beaumont Road housing estate and fronted onto North Street. The land was farmed by the Kimber family until the closure and subsequent building of the houses in the mid-1960s. Previously the farm was owned by the Stone family and Mr Thomas Parnham Stone was a sheep breeder of considerable note. In 1843 he was awarded two first prizes for sheep at the Royal Agricultural Show held at Derby.

The Old Vicarage (below left), now a private residence it was the home of the village vicar until 1946 when the present vicarage was purchased, this being situated in the High Street next to the Railway Bridge. The Old Vicarage still has a gateway through a side wall connecting it to the church.

In 1893 the Burial Board was formed to find and establish a new plot of land for use as a cemetery. Up until that time all burials had been in the churchyard. After an extensive search the present site in Cotes Road (below) was purchased and the chapel built for a sum of £1,700. The cemetery was dedicated on 30th March 1895 and the first burial of a Mrs Fanny Jacques, took place on 21st April 1895.

Old Men's Hospital

Entrance to Old Men's Hospital

Humphrey Babington Hospitals

These two buildings are still in use today for much the same purpose as was intended when they were originally built, as homes for the elderly.

As previously mentioned Humphrey Babington had such a high regard for his uncle, Theophilus Cave, that in his will of 1686 he left monies for the building of a hospital for elderly men. The occupants were to be known as 'Theophilus Cave's Bedesmen'.

The Old Men's Hospital was erected in 1694 and was to house 'six poor widowers or batchelors to be selected from amongst the aged and impotent persons of good character in Barrow and Quorndon, in the proportion of five from the former to one from the latter'.

Certain land had been laid aside in the Trust and rent from this paid for the upkeep of the premises. Increase of the annual income led to the support of five additional 'Bedesmen' in 1802. Such was the increase in revenue that a similar building to be known as the Old Women's Hospital was erected in 1825 at a total cost of £2,283.

Prior to the Second World War the 'Bedesmen' attended Sunday church service in their dark blue gowns edged in white.

In recent times the buildings have been fully modernised into self-contained flats. The Old Women's Hospital has been purchased by Charnwood Borough Council and is now totally administered by them. The income from this sale together with the sale of Pawdy Farm has enabled the Trustees to carry out the necessary alterations to the Old Men's Hospital, making accommodation now available for seven elderly men. The Trustees being under the supervision of the Charity Commissioners.

Old Women's Hospital

The River and Canal

A picturesqe view of the weir and bridge (above), which used to form part of the canal towpath until recent years. Both were probably built at the time the canal was being constructed in 1794. Prior to this there would have been a natural waterfall on the course of the river.

During the night of 22nd/23rd March 1971 the bridge and the weir collapsed causing the canal to run dry, back from Barrow Deep Lock. The weir was rebuilt but the bridge has never been replaced.

Opposite: *Two views of the mill at the lower end of Mill Lane. This mill, one of three mentioned in the* Domesday Book *as being sited in the parish, was the last to survive, being demolished in 1938, having ceased working some years prior to that date. In its early days the Mill was owned by the Lord of the Manor and all people having their corn milled left some of the flour as payment. Its final use was for the grinding of gypsum for use in cement products. The mill owner, Mr C. Goodacre brought the gypsum by barge from Nottinghamshire and then sold the finished product to local industry. The power for the mill came from two large wheels measuring 15 feet and 20 feet in diameter.*

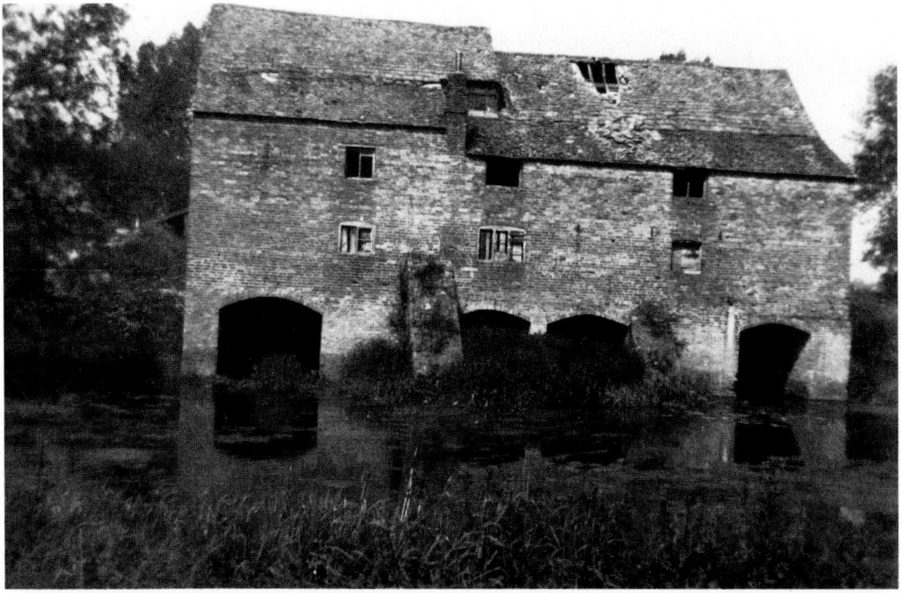

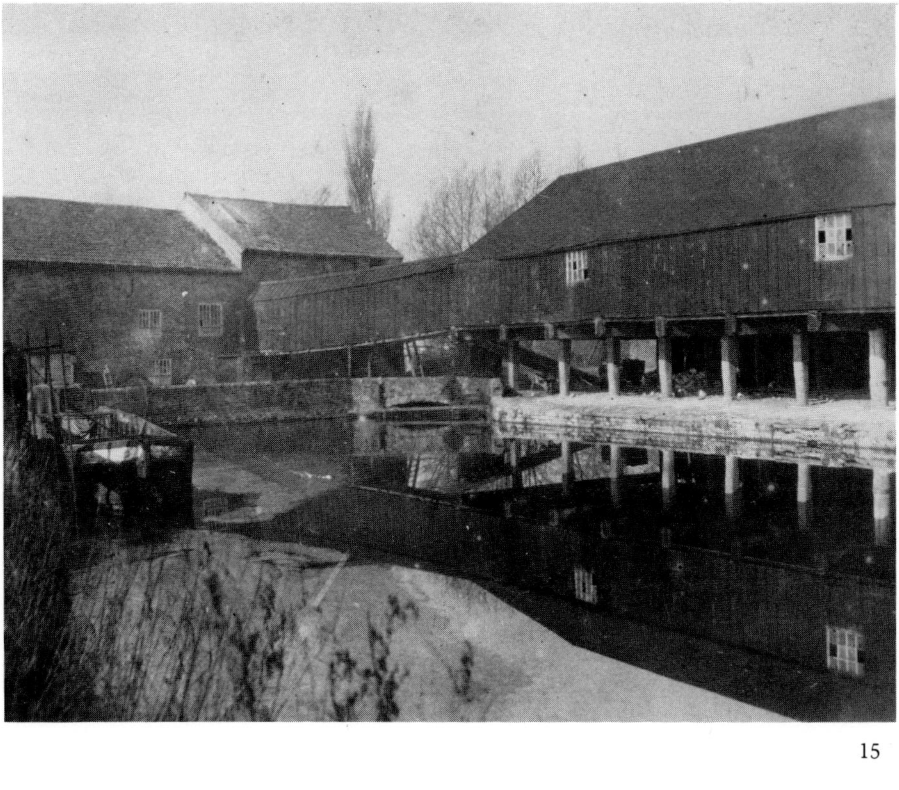

THE LOCK, BARROW-ON-SOAR.

16

Boat House, Barrow-on-Soar. Boarding, etc. Teas & Refreshments.

Boating has proved a popular pastime over many years. The photograph (above) shows rowing boats at Flint's Boat House, now the Riverside Restaurant.

The horse drawn narrow boat Kingswood (opposite, top), owned by Fellows, Morton and Clayton Ltd, Canal Carriers, negotiating the Barrow Deep Lock, circa 1905. The canal or 'cut' was built by the Leicester Navigation Co. in 1794 linking up with the Loughborough Canal which then gave direct access by water to Hull, Birmingham and London.

Barrow Bridge was built in 1845, the date can be seen on a wall plate under one of the arches. An earlier bridge, which the present one replaced, was sited slightly upstream to its present position. This one was only wide enough to accept a horse and cart with recesses built in either side for pedestrians to enter when carts were passing. The photograph clearly shows the cobbled towpath which has, with time, all but eroded away and the boatmen's 'running board' can be seen beyond the centre arch.

The Floods, Barrow on Soar. August 28th 1912.

The Floods, Barrow on Soar. August 28th 1912.

The Floods, Barrow on Soar. August 28th 1912.

The floodwater of August 28th 1912 was one of the highest recorded this century. A newspaper report at the time stated 'After a comparitively fine Sunday, rain set in at about 5.00am on Monday and the downpour continued without interruption for 15 hours'. An eye-witness report at the time stated 'This is one of the deepest floods we have known in Barrow, anyone who didn't know would never have thought there were fields here. The top step on the slabs was covered and the railings on the lane were quite out of sight'.

(The three photographs were obviously taken at different times, one clearly shows the flood at its height and later ones after they had receded somewhat.)

19

Cotes Road

Humphrey Perkins School has been on its present site since 1902 when Mr Fernsby was headmaster. The building was officially opened on the 2nd June that year and the full compliment of scholars at that time was 32 boys and one girl. Up until that time the Grammar School, as it was then known, was situated in a building which now houses the Conservative Club.

The school was founded in 1717 by Humphrey Perkins who endowed a house and farmland at Radcliffe-on-Trent, for the financial support of a master to teach the children of the parishioners of Barrow after they can read the Bible 'In all sorts of learning and free from any expense to their parents'.

At that time the Parish of Barrow extended to Quorn, Woodhouse and part of Mountsorrel, therefore the children of these villages qualified to attend.

Cotes Road *(opposite)* or Catsick Lane, as it used to be known, is also the home of the Old Board School. Built in 1880 it has served the community well, providing an education for the younger children of the village from that time until it finally closed its doors to pupils at the end of the Summer Term 1981.

COTES ROAD, BARROW-ON-SOAR.

Sports and Pastimes

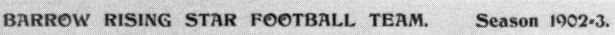

Barrow Rising Star Football Team

Barrow Rising Star football teams of 1901/2 and 1902/3 photographed (opposite), along with their trophies, on their ground. The ground was situated at the bottom of Mill Lane, over the canal bridge, in the field to the right of the lane, just as you turn left on the footpath to Mountsorrel. The 'Stars' were members of the Loughborough and District League. Those two years proved to be the high watermark of their success, winning the league championship in both seasons together with several other trophies. Following their demise came such teams as 'Barrow Trinity', 'The Gunners', 'Barrow Athletic' and, since 1932, the 'Old Boys', with a break during the Second World War.

Barrow Ladies Hockey Team

Barrow Ladies Hockey Team — 1930s. Left to right: Miss G. Allen; Miss I. Kettle; Miss I. Lee; Miss F. Allen; Miss M. Williamson; Miss L. Bowler; Miss M. Ladkin; Miss E. Oswin; Miss M. Whitehouse; Miss N. Swain and Miss I. Swain.

The hockey team played friendly games against teams from the Leicester and Loughborough areas. Their pitch was in the same field where the 'Stars' used to play. This field was also used during the summer by the village cricket team. The hockey team had their headquarters at the Baptist Chapel where this team photograph was taken.

Barrow Prize Band

The Barrow Prize Band was formed in 1847 with nine members under the leadership of Mr William Hatton. They met for practise once a week in a room opposite the now closed Fox Inn, North Street. Their first public appearance consisted of a march of about two miles along Cotes Road. In 1910 they entered competitions for a period of two years only and won contests at Melton and Derby for presentation and marching. When the First World War broke out 14 members of the band joined up, but the remainder managed to carry on until they could properly re-form in 1919.

Major Martin of The Lodge was a keen supporter of the band and when giving a piece of land in Mill Lane to the village for use as a recreation ground, he also erected a bandstand on this open space and the band played there every Feast Sunday.

Mr Sam Darby was bandmaster from the age of 17 in 1876 for a period of 50 years and on his retirement in 1926 was presented with a purse of money subscribed by the residents and his fellow bandsmen. Owing to the Second World War the band ceased playing and finally amalgamated with Sileby Band.

In the photograph are: left to right; back row: *Jack Darby, Burton, Ferrin, Foster Summers, Jack Phillips, Ginger Whiteman, Tom Sutton, Ernest Sutton, Gamble, Albert Hartsorn.* Front row: *Horace Neal, Ernest Sutton, Wells, Len Chapman, Reuben Lovett, Sam Darby (bandmaster).*

The village Church Lads Brigade on parade in the early 1900s.

The musical Bennett family taken at the rear of the Baptist Chapel. Mr R.H. Bennett Snr. on the right of the picture was, for many years, Clerk to the Parish Council and also author of the book A Short History of Barrow-upon-Soar.

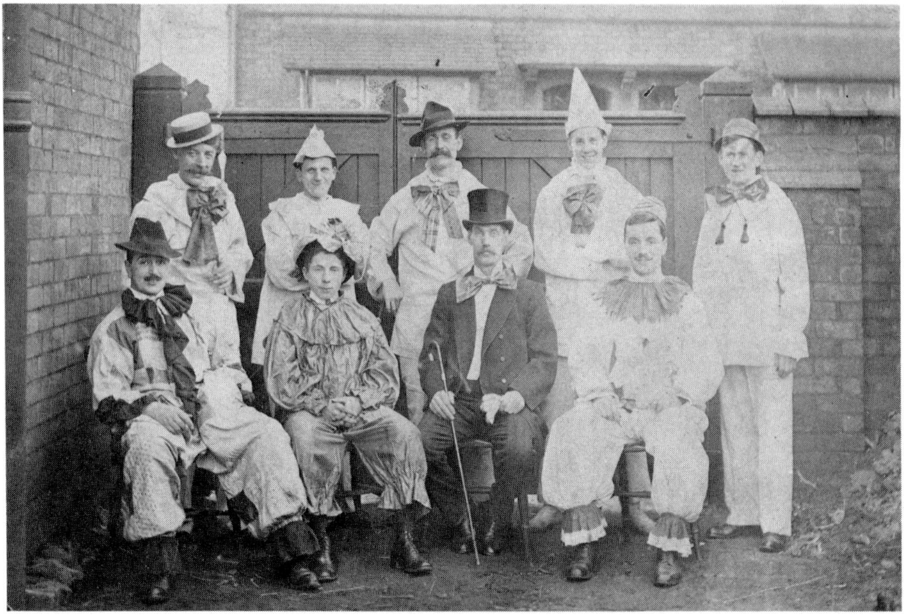

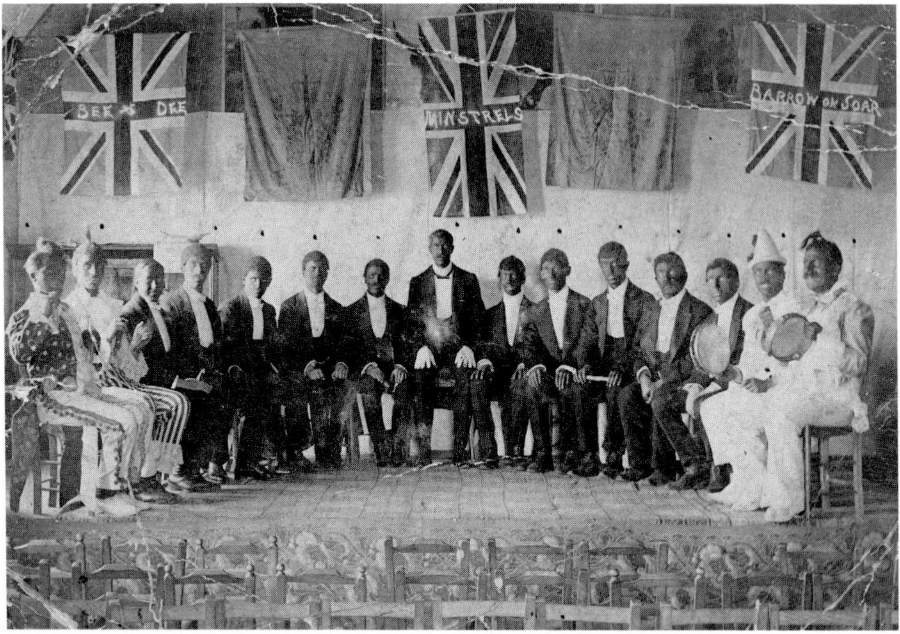
MINSTRELS
BARROW ON SOAR

One wonders what these young ladies were up to parked outside the 'Ram Inn' in The Rushes at Loughborough (now Times Caravans). Could it be a church outing, a mystery tour or just a pub crawl?

Barrow Concert Party

Barrow-upon-Soar Concert Party — 1916. This photograph was taken in the yard of the then Liberal club which is now the Working Men's Club. Left to right (back row): I. Lacey, W. Haseldine, W. Evans, R. Bennett Jnr and H. Haseldine. (Front row) E. Hardy, G. Walters, R. Bennett Snr and W Hardy. (Mr W. Evans is the gentleman who wrote the verse shown on the final page of this booklet.)

Bee and Dee Minstrels

The minstrels in the photograph were formed mainly from the employees of the hosiery factory of Black and Drivers and were known then as the 'Bee and Dee Minstrels'.

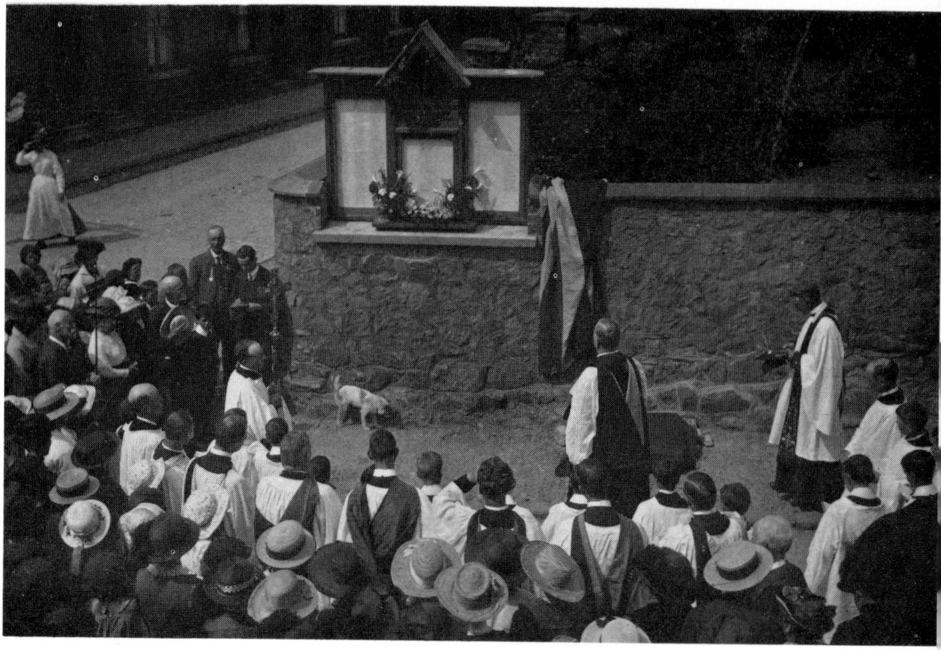

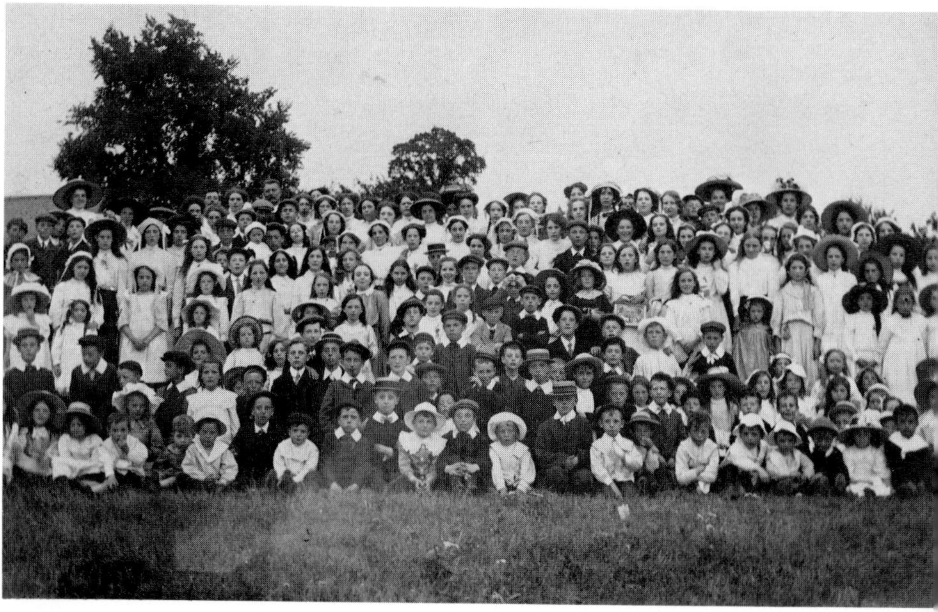

Occasions

The War Shrine (opposite, top), situated at the corner of North Street and Church Street, was erected as a memorial to those who died during the First World War. It was soon replaced by a more substantial memorial, that of the Cross, in Industry Square, which still stands.

A large group of village children (opposite, bottom) assembled to celebrate the Coronation of King George V. in 1911. One or two of our older citizens are to be seen on this photograph, and the Reverend T. Stone is the gentleman with the moustache at the back.

The bazaar in aid of the Church Organ Fund held at The Lodge, South Street on July 4th 1906. The Reverend T. Stone, then the vicar of the village, appears to be opening the fête and the other gentleman in the picture is Major Martin, owner of The Lodge, from whom comes the name Martin Avenue, which is now on part of the land once owned by him. One presumes the event was a success as an organ was acquired soon after from one of the Leicester churches.

Street Scenes

On the right hand side beyond the motor car set back from the road is a house called 'Haselmere' which in the early 1900s was the home of Mr Frank Bastert, a German and co-founder of Morris Cranes. From 1900 to 1912 the firm was known as Herbert Morris and Bastert Ltd. He was a very tough employer, exacting hard work and good time-keeping. He would walk from his home and be on the East Side Gate in Empress Road, Loughborough at 6.00 a.m. where he would lock out all latecomers. He returned to Germany prior to the First World War but his reputation lived on. When, on 31st January 1916, a bomb was dropped on the Morris Works from a German Zeppelin airship, there were those who swore they had seen Frank Bastert sneering down on them. (An unlikely story on a dark night!)

Opposite: *High Steet, known in the early 1900s as North Street. On the left is Bill Black's Post Office. The gate beyond the shop was the entrance to Mr Black's smithy. (Quite a combination, postmaster and blacksmith!)*

Some of the workforce leaving Black and Drivers factory c. 1905. This factory together with John Ellis Ltd were for many years the main employers of the working population of the village.

NEW STREET, BARROW-ON-SOAR. 620.

TOWN END, BARROW-ON-SOAR 677.

32

Above: *Beveridge Street, known originally as Industry Street, possibly because of the many handframes which were situated in numerous houses in the street for producing stockings, shirts, gloves etc, approximately 100 years ago. The street contains the oldest house in the village, Beveridge House, made of local limestone, and reputed to be some 650 years old. The house was at one time the Vicarage of Barrow and legend has it that it is linked to the church by an underground passage, a story which has yet to be proved.*

Top opposite: *New Street; built towards the end of the 19th century the street housed a small shoe factory which was burnt down in the 1920s. Houses were subsequently built on the plot. The shop in the photograph was a registered plumbers owned by W.G. Hull. Until the 1950s most of the streets in the village contained at least one 'corner shop'.*

Below opposite: *The cottages in 'Town End' stood on the site of the present Old Person's Bungalows, opposite the Lime Kiln Inn, North Street, and were known as Monkey Row. At the upper end of the row was the entrance to a field which, until recent years, was the venue for the annual 'Wakes' or fair. The Lime Kiln, known affectionately as 'The Trap', derived both of its names from the nearby limeworks which were positioned on the site of North's shop in Brook Lane. It was said to trap the men and their money on the way home from work.*

This picturesque thatched cottage once stood at the corner of North Street and Church Street. It later became the site of the village War Shrine, (a photograph of which appears on page 28). On the opposite corner of Church Street was 'The King William IV' public house which closed its doors in 1942. In 1846 there were no less than eight public houses together with nine places known as beer houses.

Opposite: *The Mount which is situated in the High Street adjacent to the railway bridge. It is one of several fine houses built in the village during the mid to late 19th century to house the local factory owners and merchants. This photograph taken in 1905 shows the owner Mrs C.S. Thomson whose husband was a wine merchant in Leicester.*

Mr and Mrs Thomson were active members of the community. Mr Thomson was elected a member of the first Parish Council on 4th December 1894, the Chairman of that council being Mr C. Goodacre, the owner of the mill. Mrs Thomson was involved, along with her husband and several other people, in raising funds for the erection of the War Memorial in Industry Square.

Above: Chestnut Avenue leading to Quorn Hall. Although not strictly in the Parish of Barrow it now provides the entrance to the Barrow Old Boys F.C. Riverside Park. Note the wrought iron railings which have now all but disappeared.

BOYHOOD DAYS
By the late William Evans

I climb again as oft I've climbed
Old Pawdy's steep, steep hill,
then looking 'cross the Valley of the Soar
I see, in the distance blue, the Beacon Hill.

There just beyond my outstretched hand
Or, so it seems to me,
My native village on the knoll
Peeps out from 'mongst the trees.

Out-topping all the old grey Church
Close by it stands the School,
Where I was taught to read and write
And many another golden rule.

Where are my playmates of those days?
They're scattered now both far and wide,
Some have sailed across the sea
Alas, alas and some have died.

And though from here I cannot see,
There is a spot more dear than all,
A cottage by the old grey mill,
And by the gate a poplar tall.

And in the fields beyond the hedge
I roamed, yes, many a day,
And sweetly sang the birds to me,
And oh how sweet the new-mown hay.

And when, at night, the mill did cease,
And through the trees the pale moon rose,
I laid me down and sweetly slept
Until the morning's sun uprose.

Ha! these were happy, happy days
I'll never tire their praise to sing,
I would not change my little cot
Not for the palace of a king.

There's many another memory dear
That I could tell that's true,
Of how I spent my boyhood's days
But this, I think, will do.

The sun sinks fast, the shadows fall,
I retrace my footsteps down the hill,
But as long as I live I'll never forget
The dear little cot that stands by the mill.